ABC DEGENERACY

by frank orchard

Aa is for abortion, killing the unborn

Bb is for brutalism, boring and forlorn

Cc is for commie cucks
and cancerous cancel culture

GETTING TO YES

Dd

is for drag queens
preying on children
like vultures

Ee is for elderly abuse, enablers and emasculation

Ff is for furries and false rape allegations

LOSER

Gg is for globalism, gambling and green hair

Hh
is for hentai
and HIV from a promiscuous affair

Ii

is for ingesting booze, drugs and cigarettes

Jj is for jerking off to incest porn on the internet

Kk is for kiddy-diddlers destroying innocent lives

Ll

is for lowlifes looting
and losers beating their wives

Mm is for marxist media and mass immigration

BREAKING: WALLS ARE RACIST

WAR IS PEACE, FREEDOM IS SLAVERY, IGNORANCE IS STRENGTH

LEMONADE 25¢

Nn is for the nanny state crippling our nation

Oo is for OnlyFans and the obsessively offended

OnlyDegenerates

$4.99

Pp is for progressivism
and prostitutes befriended

Qq is for queers marching naked down the street

IN THIS HOUSE WE BELIEVE
VIRTUE SIGNALING CHILD-LIKE IDEALS
IS MORE IMPORTANT THAN
A UNITED CULTURE
A SAFE NATION
AND OUR COUNTRYMEN'S WELLBEING

Rr is for refugees welcome
(to suckle on the taxpayer's teat)

Ss is for sodomite soyboys and shameless slutwalks

SLUT SLUT SLUT SLUT

DEGENERATES

T t

is for tattooed trannies, suicidal for losing their cocks

HERE LIES

WILLIAM

HERE LIES

WILLIAM'S WILLY

Uu is for undesirable, ugly on the inside, ugly on the out

Vv

is for victimhood and virtue-signaling for internet clout

Ww

Women's Studies

Way to go.

is for women's studies and whining about oppression

Xx is for XXX causing isolation and depression

Yy is for youths without fathers, yearning masculinity

Zz is for zero culture and zero responsibility

Thank you for reading!

If this journey delighted (or sickened) you,
please share a review where you bought it.

Also by Frank Orchard:

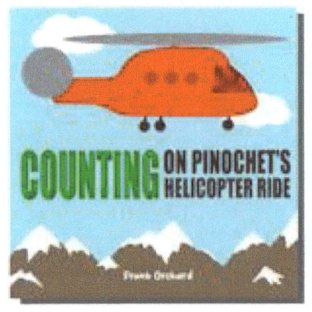